SEPAR*ATIONS*

DEATH

■

by Janine Amos
Illustrated by Gwen Green
Photographs by Angela Hampton

■

Gareth Stevens Publishing
A WORLD ALMANAC EDUCATION GROUP COMPANY

Please visit our web site at: **www.garethstevens.com**
For a free color catalog describing Gareth Stevens Publishing's list of high-quality books
and multimedia programs, call 1-800-542-2595 or fax your request to (414) 332-3567.

Library of Congress Cataloging-in-Publication Data

Amos, Janine.
    Death / text by Janine Amos; illustrations by Gwen Green; photography by
Angela Hampton.
      p. cm. — (Separations)
    Includes bibliographical references.
    Summary: Uses letters, stories, and informational text to help children cope with
the death of a loved one.
    ISBN 0-8368-3089-X (lib. bdg.)
    1. Children and death—Juvenile literature. [1. Death.] I. Green, Gwen, ill.
II. Hampton, Angela, ill. III. Title.
BF723.D3A58   2002
155.9'37—dc21   2001054948

This edition first published in 2002 by
Gareth Stevens Publishing
A World Almanac Education Group Company
330 West Olive Street, Suite 100
Milwaukee, WI 53212 USA

This U.S. edition © 2002 by Gareth Stevens, Inc. First published in 1997 by Cherrytree
Press, a subsidiary of Evans Brothers Limited. © 1997 by Cherrytree (a member of the
Evans Group of Publishers), 2A Portman Mansions, Chiltern Street, London W1M 1LE,
United Kingdom. This U.S. edition published under license from Evans Brothers Limited.
Additional end matter © 2002 by Gareth Stevens, Inc.

Gareth Stevens cover design and page layout: Tammy Gruenewald
Gareth Stevens series editor: Dorothy L. Gibbs

Printed in the United States of America

1 2 3 4 5 6 7 8 9 06 05 04 03 02

Contents

Letters: Dear Grandma — Dear Sam   4

Story: Hannah's Birthday   6

Letters: Dear Auntie Fran — Dear Judy   12

Feelings: When Someone Dies   14

How to Help Yourself Cope   16

Letters: Dear Grandma — Dear Sam   18

Feelings: Better or Worse?   20

Helping Yourself Move On   22

Story: Dad's Special Book   24

Letters: Dear Auntie Fran — Dear Judy   30

More Books to Read — Web Sites   32

Dear Grandma,

I wish you had a phone. I really want to talk to you. Mom says you're coming to stay with us soon. Please hurry up and come.

I can't believe Dad is dead. I want it to be a lie. He was a good driver. How could he crash into a truck? Why wasn't he concentrating? The stupid truck driver must have been going too fast.

Dad promised he was going to teach me to play chess this summer, but now he can't. It's not fair. I'll never learn how to play chess.

I didn't say goodbye to Dad that day before he went to work. I was still in bed, and he yelled at me to get up. Maybe he was angry with me? Maybe that made him crash? I wish I had said goodbye. I wish he would come back.

Everything's spinning around in my head. Why did this have to happen to my dad?

All these people are at our house. No one knows what to say. I want them to go away. Mom doesn't have time for me anymore. I don't want to see my friends. I hate them. I hate myself. I just want to stay in my room. I feel like shouting.

Please come soon.

Love,
Sam

Dear Sam,

I'm writing back right away. It sounds as if you're very angry at the moment. You're right, it's not fair that your dad has died. It's awful and terrible, and there's nothing anyone can do to change it. No wonder you feel like shouting. Why don't you try punching a pillow or kicking a football really hard? It might help a little when you feel really bad.

I'm coming next Tuesday to stay for as long as you and your mom need me. We can talk as much as you like then, or we can just be together.

Your dad's crash was an accident, Sam. Nothing you did made it happen. We'll never know exactly what really did happen. The police said the road was icy, and both drivers lost control.

You will learn to play chess, if you want to. We'll put our heads together and think of someone who can teach you.

See you on Tuesday.

All my love,
Grandma

5

Hannah's Birthday

It was Hannah's birthday. Today, Hannah would normally bounce out of bed. She would be the first one up, so she could get the morning mail. Then she would tear open her birthday cards and rush to open her presents.

On this birthday, however, Hannah didn't feel like getting up at all. She stayed in bed with the curtains closed. Just one week ago, Hannah's grandma had died. Hannah clenched her hands into fists and squeezed her eyes tightly shut. "Why did Grandma die before my party?" thought Hannah, angrily. She punched her pillow hard. "Why did she have to die now?"

At breakfast, Hannah's mom tried to be cheerful. She was planning the food for Hannah's party.

"Come on, Hannah," she said brightly. "Eat your breakfast so we can go into town to buy the pizzas."

But Hannah couldn't eat.

"I've got a tummy ache, right in the middle," she said.

Hannah's mom sat down next to her.

"I know how much you're missing Grandma," she said gently. "But she was very old. She couldn't live forever."

Hannah banged her fist on the table. "But I didn't want her to die!" she shouted.

Hannah's mom went into town by herself. Hannah wandered into the living room. Her dad was there. He had tears streaming down his face. Hannah felt funny. She had never seen her dad cry before, not even at the funeral.

"I was just thinking about Grandma," he murmured.

Hannah put her head down and twisted her heel into the carpeting.

"Why did Grandma have to die now?" she asked. "I wanted her to be here for my party."

"She'd be here if she could," Hannah's dad replied. He smiled a little bit. "Your grandma loved parties."

Hannah looked at her dad.

"She was sad to leave you," he went on, "but she was so tired, Hannah."

Hannah nodded. "I knew that," she said. "I know that old people have to die. It's still horrible though, isn't it?"

"Yes," Hannah's dad agreed quietly.

"Mom went to get the party food," said Hannah. "She wants me to have a happy birthday."

Her dad looked at her.

"It's hard to be happy when you feel sad inside," he said.

They didn't say anything else for a long time. Hannah listened to the "tick-tock" of the old clock. Then she remembered something.

"I haven't opened my present from Grandma yet. It's in my room."

"Let's go!" said her dad, holding out his hand.

Hannah's dad sat on her bed. Hannah stood on tiptoes to get a large package down from the shelf.

"Grandma said it was something special," said Hannah as she carefully opened the shiny wrapping paper. Inside was a beautiful, deep-blue velvet party dress.

"Oh!" gasped Hannah. "Grandma knew I liked this dress, but I didn't think she'd get it for me."

"It looks like Grandma wanted you to have a happy birthday, too," said Hannah's dad, smiling.

Dear Auntie Fran,

Katy's dead, but I don't feel sad. I know I should. My only sister has died, but I can't cry. When I see Mom and Dad crying, I feel so bad. I'm looking forward to things getting back to normal. No more rushing to the hospital in the middle of the night. No more tiptoeing around in the afternoon so we don't wake up Katy. No more waiting for Katy to die.

I'm scared. I wonder if I'll die soon, too. I've got a stomachache like Katy had, but Mom and Dad don't listen. My stomach feels worse at night. It's so sore it keeps me awake. That's when I get scared.

Please write to me soon.

Lots of love,

Judy

Dear Judy,
    Thanks for writing to me. It's been such a difficult time for all of you. No wonder you're hoping things will get better soon. It's natural to feel the way you do. It doesn't mean you didn't love Katy. But it might be a long time before everything gets better.
    You're all feeling sad, and when people are so sad, their feelings come out in different ways. Your mom and dad are crying a lot because they miss Katy so much. But it doesn't mean they don't love you. They do! You sound like you're all mixed up inside. Maybe that's why your stomach hurts. It's your way of being sad.
    Try to tell your mom and dad how you feel, or maybe you could talk to a teacher you like. If you talk about it, in time, your stomachache will go away.
    A big hug,
    Auntie Fran

13

Feelings: When Someone Dies

When someone special dies, it's natural to have all kinds of feelings. Some of them you might not understand.

■ People die for all kinds of reasons. Often, very old people die because their bodies are tired and worn out. Sometimes young people die, too. They get sick, and, no matter how hard doctors try to help them, nothing makes them better. They are too ill to stay alive. Some people get killed in accidents. No matter how a person dies, death is the end of life. Someone who dies can never come back to life again.

■ When someone special dies, you might have lots of different feelings. At times, some feelings will be stronger than others, and they can be scary.

■ One feeling might be very deep sadness. Some children get so sad that it's hard for them to know what they're feeling. They get stomachaches, like Judy, or feel sick.

■ Sam feels angry — at his dad for dying and at the truck driver. Like Sam, you might feel angry at the person who died, at yourself, or at everyone! You might even feel angry at families who haven't had anyone die. It doesn't seem fair.

Some children find it hard to believe that the special person is really dead. It seems like a bad dream. Some children don't feel anything at all. They are numb.

All of these feelings are natural, and they are all OK. A lot of children have many fears and worries when someone special dies. Many of them worry that they caused the death somehow. They wonder if, by thinking or doing something bad, they made that person die. Nothing they might have said or done would have caused the person to die.

When a special person dies, some children fear for the safety of other people in their family. They worry that someone else they love will die suddenly, so they don't want to let those people out of their sight. Judy is worried that she will die now, like her sister.

Sometimes after a death in the family, nothing seems to make sense anymore. You might feel all mixed up. Your parents might be feeling this way, too. That's why it's often hard to help each other. Is there anyone else who could come to be with all of you at this time?

How to Help Yourself Cope

When someone special dies, it's natural to feel angry, frightened, sad, and confused. Here are some ways you can help yourself at this time:

- Say goodbye to the person you loved and who loved you. Ask to go to the funeral or the special service. If going to the funeral or service isn't possible, say goodbye in your own special way. Perhaps you could spend a little bit of quiet time in your room looking at a photograph of the person who died.

- Remember that it's not your job to make other people feel better. You can't take the place of someone who has died, either. It's hard enough to take care of yourself when you feel so upset.

- Having someone — or something, such as a pet — to talk to might help. Talking won't change what has happened, but it can help you feel better.

Don't expect to feel better right away. You'll have good times and bad times — but that's OK. You might feel like doing things you stopped doing a long time ago, such as taking a bottle to bed with you. Asking to do these things is all right.

You might like to have your own special photograph of the person who died — one that is just for you. Don't be afraid to ask for it.

Don't be afraid to ask questions, either. You might need to know more about the death than you've been told. If your parents find it hard to give you answers, try talking to another adult you trust. If you don't understand, keep asking people questions.

Remember that laughing and having fun are still OK. You don't have to be sad all the time. Remember, too, that you're not alone. A lot of people care about you.

Don't forget! Nothing you thought or said or did caused this special person to die.

17

Dear Grandma,

Guess what? I can play chess. My friend Jason's dad has been teaching us every night after school.

I won a prize at school for my photography. It was in a big competition. You had to take a picture of someone in your family. I took lots of pictures of Mom and some of myself, but when I got the film developed, the best pictures were some old ones I took of Dad in his running clothes. It made me feel funny to see them. I had forgotten they were in the camera. Mom said that a photo of Dad would still count, even though he's dead, so I sent in one.

Mrs. Franey gave me the prize in front of the whole school. The photo is on my bedroom wall now, in a big frame. Sometimes it makes me feel sad, but I like it being there. It's sort of like my dad is still around.

I went to school camp last week. I stayed away for two nights, but I missed Mom. I told Mr. Brook, my teacher, and he let me phone her both days. The next day I wanted to go home, but Mr. Brook says I can go to camp again next year anyway.

Love,
Sam

18

Dear Sam,

I enjoyed hearing from you. Congratulations on learning to play chess and for winning the photography prize. Your Dad would have been very proud of you.

I'd love to have a copy of that photo. Would you be able to get one made for me? It's always nice to have a special photograph to help us remember.

Do you remember the first camera your dad bought you? You were only four, and everyone said you were too young to take pictures. But your Dad loved photography, and he thought you would, too. He was right, wasn't he? You're like him in lots of ways.

I'm glad you got to go to camp. I bet you're looking forward to next year.

Thinking of you.

Love,

Grandma

Feelings: Better or Worse?

Even a long time after a special person has died, you might still feel sad and confused. You might also get angry with yourself that you don't feel better. All of these feelings are natural.

■ Sometimes children find it hard to do things with their friends after someone special has died. They might get angry easily and shout or pick fights. Months, or even years, after the death of a special person, some children are still afraid to be away from their families. That's why Sam wanted to come home from camp. Big changes, such as moving or going to a new school, can be especially scary.

■ Some children find it hard to go on with everyday life when someone they love has died. They have good days when they can laugh and play, but they also have days when the bad feelings come back. Then, it's as if the person they loved has just died.

If your mom or dad has died, your living parent might, after a while, come to love a new partner. Many children find a situation like this difficult. They worry that it isn't being kind to the parent who died. Remember that nothing can take away the love you shared with a parent who has died. That love is yours to keep forever.

It's OK to feel sad, angry, and frightened when someone you loved has died. The death of a special person is painful, too. This pain is called grief, and it is part of saying goodbye to that person. Take as long as you need to grieve.

The Death of a Pet

The first time you learn about death might be when your pet dies. Finding out that you will never see your pet again might feel like the end of the world to you. Try to remember that pets and people can stay with us in our memories. This way, they are part of our lives forever.

21

Helping Yourself Move On

If you're finding it hard to go on with your life after someone special has died, here are some things you can do to help yourself:

■ Visit a place that makes you think of the person who died. This place might be the person's grave or somewhere the person liked to be when he or she was alive. It might be somewhere you had fun together. It can become the special place where you spend time thinking about the person who died.

■ If you have a garden, you could grow a rose, or some other plant, that will bloom in years to come and help you remember the person you loved.

■ Draw pictures or write about how you feel. Bad feelings can seem less powerful when you put them down on paper. You might even want to rip up what you draw or write, afterward. It's up to you.

At times, when you're feeling especially upset, it helps to be with someone you know well. If you feel bad, try spending some time with someone you trust until you're feeling good again. Talking a lot about the person who died might make you feel better, too.

Even a long time after someone has died, people sometimes still need to cry about it. Remember, it takes time to say goodbye to someone you loved. The right amount of time for you is however long it takes.

Dad's Special Book

Plop! "There he goes," whispered Richard. Jack looked over to where his stepfather was pointing, just in time to catch sight of a muskrat's furry body. As the muskrat slipped into the water, Jack smiled. He was having fun. He liked Richard. Richard didn't keep talking all the time or asking Jack questions. He showed Jack what to look for and pointed things out. So far, they had seen two muskrats and a kingfisher and had shared a whole package of ginger cookies.

At four o'clock it was time to pack up.

"Race you back to the campsite!" said Richard.

Off they went, scrambling up the steep slope. They reached the top side by side and puffing. Jack's mom was sitting in the sun, reading a book. They flopped down beside her. Richard gently tugged the book away.

"Peace is over for now," he laughed. "The boys are back!" He held the book up high in one hand.

Jack grinned. "I'll get it, Mom!" he said, grabbing Richard's legs in a football tackle.

Soon they were rolling around on the grass — Mom, too. Richard was ticklish, and he laughed in loud chuckles. Jack liked the way Richard's eyes crinkled at the corners. He remembered how his dad's eyes had been like that.

Suddenly, Jack pulled away. He got up and ran inside the tent. Mom and Richard stopped laughing, and Jack could feel them watching him.

"Hey! What's the matter?" Richard called out.

But Jack couldn't answer him. The tent was hot inside, so Jack kicked off his shoes. Lying down on his sleeping bag, he opened his backpack and pulled out a photograph that was in a green leather case. He stared hard at the picture. It was a picture of his dad. He had died three years ago. Jack closed his eyes and tried to see the face in his mind. He couldn't.

After a while, Jack's mom poked her head into the tent.

"Can I come in?" she asked quietly.

Jack shrugged. His mom crawled into the tent.

"Remember going camping with Dad?" asked Jack.

"I do," said his mom, smiling. "Remember when Dad put up the new tent and . . ."

"It fell down!" Jack finished. They grinned at each other.

"We've got a photograph of that somewhere," Jack's mom went on.

Jack put his head down and looked at his dad's picture.

"I'm scared I'm forgetting him," he whispered.

"I know," said his mom. "But we've got lots of good memories of Dad. Nothing can ever take those away. They're part of our life."

"Do you think Dad would mind us having fun with Richard?" Jack asked slowly.

His mom shook her head. "He wouldn't mind," she said. "Having fun with Richard can't spoil any of the good times we had with Dad."

"Do you know where that tent photo is?" asked Jack.

"Yes," said his mom. "Why don't we make a scrapbook when we get home? Full of all the special things we remember about Dad? We can put that photo in for a start."

Two weeks later, Jack and his mom sat in Jack's room. Balanced on their knees was a fat scrapbook full of pictures, photographs, football programs, and some writing about Jack's dad. Jack and his mom had made the scrapbook together.

Jack patted the book. "It's really big," he said. "I didn't think I remembered so much."

Then Jack saw Richard standing at the door.

"Come and see our scrapbook," said Jack.

Richard sat down next to them as Jack slowly turned the pages.

"Wow," said Richard, when they reached the end. "You certainly had some fun together, you three."

"We did," said Jack, smiling at him.

Dear Auntie Fran,

Yesterday was Katy's birthday. She would have been ten years old. It was really sad. I was crying at school. I didn't go out at recess time. I talked to my teacher about it, and I decided to draw Katy a picture as a kind of birthday present. I put in all the things Katy liked best — ice cream, skating, dancing, the Spice Girls, cats, Mom, Dad, and me. I put the picture in Katy's bedroom. It made me feel better. At dinner, Mom, Dad, and I said "Happy Birthday" to Katy.

I miss her every day and most of all on weekends. We used to do each other's hair and goof around. Last weekend, my friend Sophie came to stay overnight. She has a ponytail. It was nice to have someone to play with, but she's not the same as Katy.

Lots of love,
Judy

Dear Judy,

    It was great to get a letter from you.

    I remembered it was Katy's birthday.

I spent some time thinking about those dances she showed us. We had great fun, didn't we? Remember when she first taught us to jazz dance? We got our feet all tangled up, and we fell over!

    It's nice that Sophie stayed with you for the weekend. I bet you had a lot of fun. Do you want to bring her here with you when you come?

    See you then.

    Love,

    Auntie Fran

31

More Books to Read

- *A Child's Simple Guide through Grief*.
  Alexis Cunningham
  (Jalmar Press)

- *Geranium Morning: A Book about Grief*.
  E. Sandy Powell
  (Lerner Publications)

- *I Don't Have an Uncle Phil Anymore*.
  Marjorie White Pellegrino
  (Magination Press)

- *Rudi's Pond*.
  Eve Bunting
  (Houghton Mifflin)

Web Sites

- The National Center for Grieving Children & Families:
  GrievingChild.org.
  www.dougy.org/kid.html

- When Somebody Dies.
  kidshealth.org/kid/feeling/emotion/somedie.html